AN AMAZING
ALPHABET

By John Patience

© Published by Peter Haddock Limited, Bridlington, U.K.

Printed in Singapore

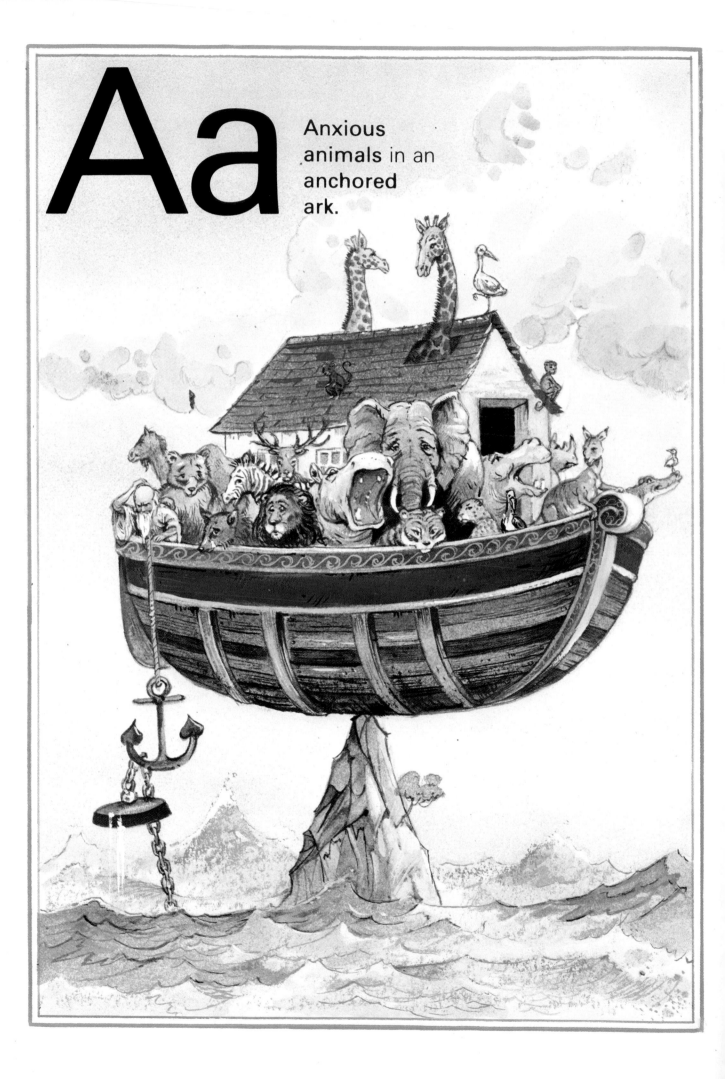

Aa

Anxious animals in an anchored ark.

Busy
baker with a
batch of
bread - oops!
banana skin.

Bb

David and the dainty dragon dancing in the daisies.

Dd

Ee Enormous elephant eating eggs.

Fairies,
flowers,
feather and
frog.

Ff

Gg

Goose
girl
greeting
gentle
giant.

Hasty hare helping himself to honey from a hive.

Hh

Ii

Indian
imagining
incredible
ice-cream.

Jj

Jolly
jester
juggling
jellies.

Kk

Kitten catching the kind king's kite.

Large
lion and
little lizard
licking
lollipops.

Ll

Mm

Moon,
mushroom and
many
merry-making
mice.

Nn

Nest of
noisy
nightingales.

Oo

One
odd
old
owl.

Parrot perching on the peg-legged pirate.

Pp

Qq

Queasy
queen
quarrelling with
quacky duck.

Rr

Rhinoceros in a rocking chair reading to a robin.

Ss

Sailor
shrews
sail the
salty seas.

Trolls gathering **tasty** **treats** for their tea.

Tt

Uu

Unusual
unicorn
under an
umbrella.

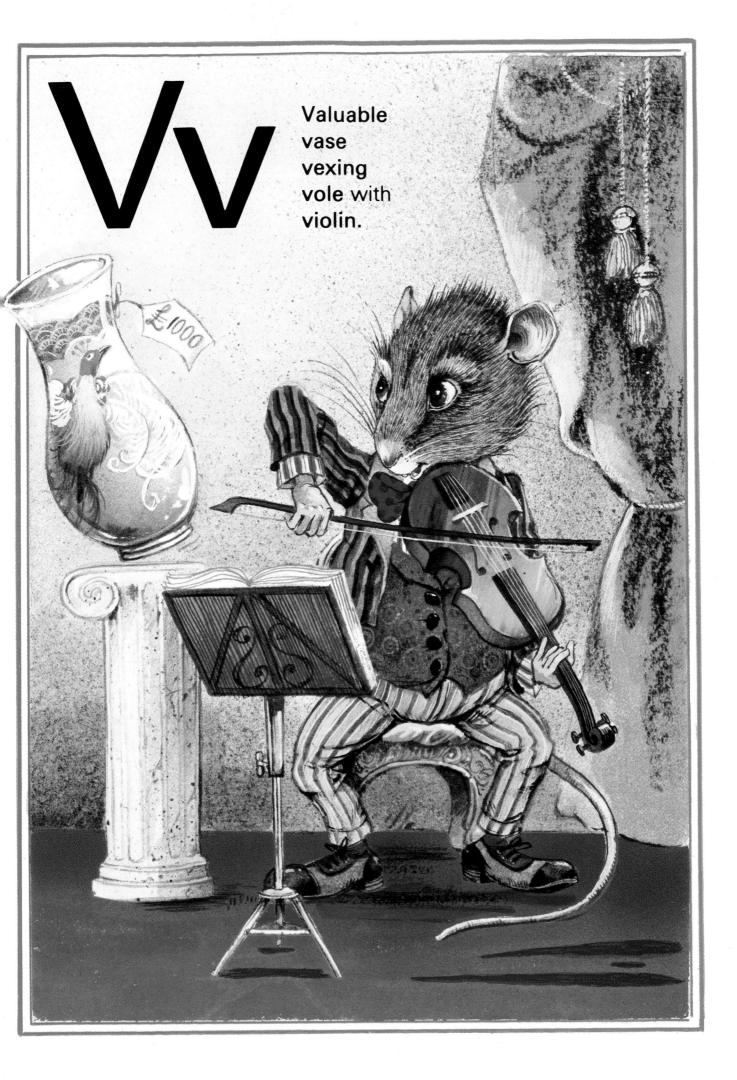

Vv

Valuable
vase
vexing
vole with
violin.

Ww

Witch and wizard waving wands.

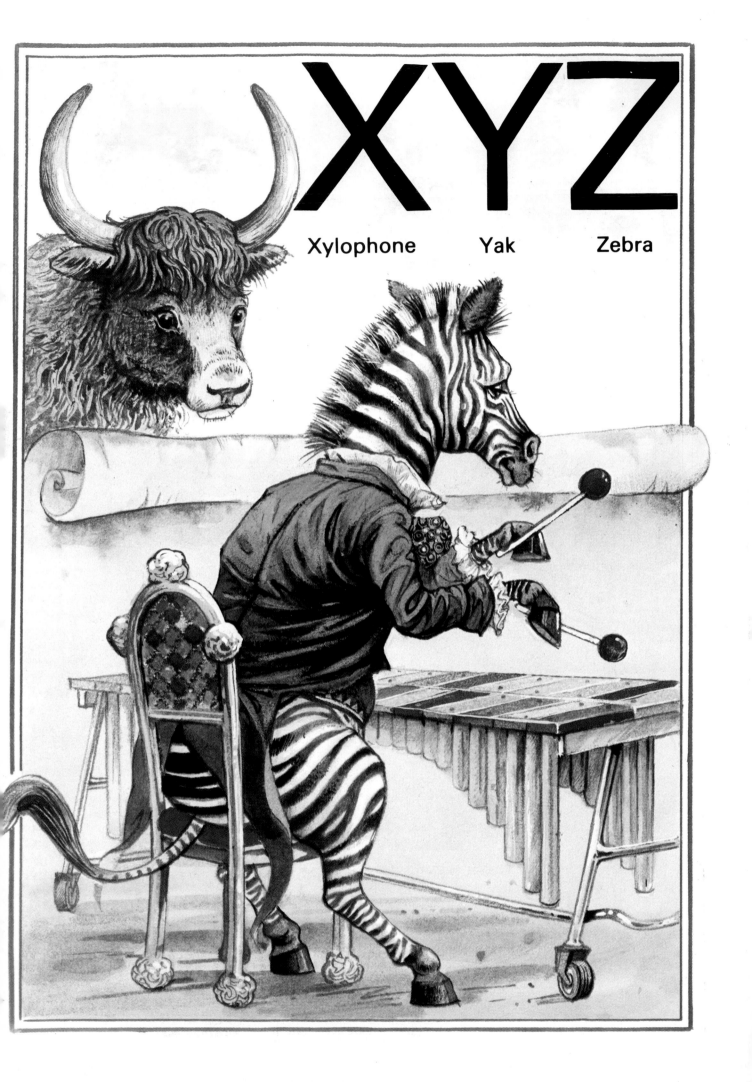

XYZ

Xylophone   Yak   Zebra